I Am Queen Nzinga
THE GREAT QUEEN WARRIOR

By Amina Phelps
Illustrated by Afzal Khan

Copyright © 2020 by Amina Phelps. All rights reseerved under International and Pan-American copyright Conventions.

1Brick Publishing, LLC, 2020. All rights reserved
Published by 1Brick Publishing. No part of this book may be reproduced or copied in any form without written permission from the copyright owner

Printed in the USA
ISBN: 978-1-949303-10-0

Long ago in a land far away, across many oceans in southwestern Africa there lived a young girl named Nzinga. She was the daughter of King Kulanji and his second wife Kangela in a country known today as Angola.

It was customary for Kings to have more than one wife however only the first wife held the title of Queen.

Although Nzinga was not the daughter of the Queen she was her father's most favored child and he took her everywhere he went.

Along with her brother Mbandi, who was being groomed to become King, Nzinga learned archery, hunting skills and was educated in politics and trade.

Nzinga enjoyed observing her father as he ruled the land and went to battle with the Portuguese.

Mbandi on the other hand was lazy and not as interested.

"Mbandi how do you expect to one day take father's place as King if you do not pay attention!" Nzinga exclaimed to her brother as he ignored his lessons.

"Nzinga I will be just fine I'm sure father will get rid of these foreigners before I'm old enough to be King and everything will be back to normal." sighed Mbandi

"Besides why are you worried? These matters are none of your concern you should be somewhere learning to cook and clean" Mbandi said sarcastically.

"I worry because if the throne is handed to you our lives will be in danger. Hopefully the people of the kingdom will recognize who the real smart one is and crown me King instead" Nzinga replied.

"Silly child you cannot be King you're a girl. Even if you were a boy you would never have a chance at the throne. Did you forget your mother is not Queen? You have no rights and would never be accepted as heir to anything" Mbandi shot back as he ran off with his friends.

This made Nzinga mad and more determined to learn everything there was to know about ruling the kingdom.

One of the tools King Kulanji used to teach the children about rule and strategy was Chess. Every evening after dinner Nzinga and her father would sit under the tree to play the game.

It was her dad's favorite game but neither she nor Mbandi liked it very much. Somehow Mbandi always cleverly found a way to get out of his session.

"Father I do not want to play, this game it's so frustrating and I never win" Nzinga sighed.

"That is exactly why I summon you to play with me my child" said the King as he eyed his next move. Even though you're frustrated and continue to lose you never give up you possess a determination that I admire.

"Well why won't you allow me to win out of the kindness of your heart" Nzinga replied.

The King laughed "If I just let you win you will never understand the game besides I want you to strengthen your thinking skills. Nzinga use your brain; before each move think about what each piece does and the power it has; at the same time, be aware of what my men are doing... Checkmate!"

Nzinga took the King's advice and began to study the game. While spending the day with her father she would pretend the noblemen and warriors were chess pieces and played the game mentally using the Portuguese as the opposing team. Little did she know this child's play would make her one of the greatest Queens of her time.

Some years had passed and King Kulanji had grown very ill. Doctors and healers gave him the best treatments but there was nothing they could do to restore his health and strength. This made Nzinga really sad and she stayed by his bedside day and night to ensure his comfort.

Before he died he told Nzinga in a weak raspy voice "Although it is my wish to crown you Queen and ruler of the Kingdom I can not. Your brother will rule but please guide him and promise to protect our people and land from the Portuguese traders."

"I promise she said as long as I am alive they will not conquer our land!"

And so Nzinga's brother Mbandi became King and as promised she supported him during his reign.

Although Mbandi and Nzinga received the same training as children Mbandi was an awful leader. He relied heavily on his sister for guidance but even with her guidance the neighboring tribes would constantly invade Ndongo.

One day the Ndongo Kingdom was under attack but instead of Mbandi fighting back he fled the country leaving the people of the land to fend for themselves.

Nzinga was unaware of her brother fleeing until she received his message requesting that she negotiate a peace treaty. The messenger said that if she was successful he would hand over the throne and make her ruler of the Ndongo and Matamba kingdoms.

Nzinga was successful and Mbandi was never seen or heard from again.

For more than 30 years Queen Nzinga successfully reigned over the two kingdoms.

Historical Fact #1

Nzinga used her wit, knowledge of politics and strategy to protect the people of the Ndongo Kingdom from Portuguese rule.

Historical Fact #2

She even went as far as adopting their religion and getting baptized to become allies with Portugal.

By doing this she gained a partner against her enemies and was able to build a stronger kingdom.

Historical Fact #3

Queen Anna Nzinga (circa 1581-1663) of Angola fought against the slave trade and European influence in the seventeenth century. Known for being an astute diplomat and visionary military leader, she resisted Portuguese invasion and slave raids for 30 years.

Historical Fact #4

A skilled negotiator, she allied herself with the Dutch and pitted them against the Portuguese in an effort to wrestle free of Portuguese domination. She fought for a free Angola until her death at age 82, after which weak rulers left the country open for the Portuguese to regain control.

Historical Fact #5

When Queen Nzinga was born the umbilical cord was wrapped around her neck. Ironically Mbundu culture viewed this as a sign of strength and determination and a woman predicted that the child would one day be Queen.

Historical Fact #6

The Mbundu people called their Kings Ngola's which is why the Portuguese ended up calling the country Angola after colonization.